Branding and People Management: What's in a name?

Dr Graeme Martin

Professor Phillip Beaumont

First published 2003

Cover design by Curve
Designed and typeset by Paperweight
Printed in Great Britain by Short Run Press

British Library Cataloguing in Publication Data:
A catalogue record for this book is available from the British Library

ISBN 1 84398 011 8

Chartered Institute of Personnel and Development
CIPD House, Camp Road, London, SW19 4UX

Tel.: 020 8971 9000
Fax: 020 8263 3333
E-mail: publish@cipd.co.uk

incorporated by Royal Charter: Registered charity no. 1079797.

Contents

Foreword

In the so-called 'weightless economy', brand has become the critical source of competitive advantage for many organisations. The production of physical output is not as important for these businesses as the brand concept.

This emphasis on developing and sustaining brand stems from the huge success that companies have had in using brand to breed consumer loyalty for core products as well as new, diversified lines of business. Supermarkets such as Tesco and Sainsbury's now sell financial services, and the Virgin brand incorporates products and services varying from soft drinks to train travel.

This report investigates whether, and how, the growing importance of brand affects the way that people are managed and developed for organisational performance. The study – which was conducted by Graeme Martin, Heriot-Watt University, and Professor Phil Beaumont, Glasgow University, on behalf of the CIPD – explores the relationship between branding and people management. It looks beyond the concept of 'employer of choice', to help people management and development specialists better understand the brand management process and their critical part in managing brand.

The authors review a range of management literature, pulling together the messages from different disciplines. They also use two case studies – Agilent Technologies and the Abbey National Group – to illustrate some of the benefits that organisations can gain from considering the employment proposition to be integral to the corporate brand.

- Agilent, a spin-off from Hewlett-Packard, has been a leading proponent of the employment brand for many years, and has made a well-publicised attempt to maintain its strong brand in difficult trading conditions.

- Abbey National is currently developing a consistent and measurable employment proposition across the Group. It has taken an evidence-based approach, including commissioning academic work on the effects of this proposition on financial advisers.

Martin and Beaumont conclude that HR strategies are intimately linked to how brand – particularly at the corporate level – is valued by customers and employees. These strategies include the extent to which the organisation sees its workforce as a driver of business success, how successfully it seeks to be an employer of choice, and how effectively it communicates the employer brand identity to its employees. The report stresses that the relationship between HR and corporate brand is mediated by the extent to which employees perceive the brand proposition to match reality, and by the brand reputation – the past ability of the company to deliver its promised outcomes.

The report outlines stages of development in the brand and HR relationship, starting from branding as a logo for products or services, with little or no input from the HR function, to corporate brand at the centre of strategy with HR in a pivotal role.

We hope that this research will help people management and development professionals engage in the strategic debate on brand management in their organisations, and understand the key role that they can play in developing and promoting brand.

Diane Sinclair

Lead adviser on public policy, CIPD

Executive summary

- This report examines the relationship between the brand management process and the way that people are managed and developed in organisations. It reviews a wealth of literature across different disciplines, and draws together common messages to illustrate the critical role of people strategies in managing brand. The study was designed to fill the gap in existing research in this area, which largely does not consider in detail the importance of people management and development policies and practices in promoting and sustaining brands.

- The report also includes two case studies (of Agilent Technologies and Abbey National) which describe the steps some companies have taken to maintain their brand images through their employment propositions – in the case of Agilent, in difficult economic conditions.

- Chapter 1 sets the context for the work by discussing the importance of branding and people management strategies in today's economy, due in particular to the growth of the service sector. It sets out the reasons, based on previous evidence, why HR practitioners must be engaged in brand management.

- The varying ways that brand is defined are examined in Chapter 2. This shows the importance that has been attributed to the internal, as well as external, role of brand. The authors argue that the shift away from product brands towards corporate-level brand and corporate reputation management has increased the need for people management issues to be taken into account in the branding process.

- A review of the literature from four different streams of work is outlined, covering literature on culture-excellence, strategic management, the concept of employer of choice, and employment branding. Recent work in the culture-excellence school of thought – which began with *In Search of Excellence* by Peters and Waterman (1982) – shows the importance of the alignment of senior management's vision for the organisation with that understood by employees. It also stresses the need for organisations to apply the values extolled by their brand, and for their external image to match that aspired to by senior managers.

- The literature on strategic management, or the 'resource-based view' of the firm, argues that organisations gain competitive advantage through their unique combination of resources – which cannot be copied – with people as the most important asset. Most recently, work in this field has focused on core competencies, and the 'balanced scorecard' approach, which has stressed the need to balance the satisfaction of external demands and the management of internal processes and people. This demonstrates the importance of linking external marketing needs with people management and development, as illustrated by the employee–customer service–profit chain. Employee behaviour is thus shown to play a critical role in promoting brand loyalty.

- Literature on the employer of choice became more popular in the 1990s, as the 'war for talent' hit the headlines. The employer of choice concept was based on research concerned with the psychological contract – the unwritten promises and expectations that form the basis of the employment relationship. An understanding of this idea has led to some organisations reviewing their commitment to staff and the values on which the employment relationship is based.

◘ The employment branding literature is concerned with the need for employees to 'live the brand'. This is centred on engaging employee loyalty to the brand and developing commitment to the organisation. A list of do's and don'ts is included for HR professionals who want to develop the employment brand in their organisations. The report argues that it is critical for the HR function to develop a compelling story for existing and potential employees about working for the organisation.

◘ Chapter 3 discusses two case studies, Agilent Technologies and Abbey National, based on company material and interviews with senior HR staff in these organisations. The case studies show that there is no one best way of managing brand and people, because different relationships between the two are required for different contexts. They also demonstrate that developing an employer of choice strategy can have enormous benefits in terms of employee commitment and alignment behind the brand.

◘ The success of the policies pursued by Agilent Technologies illustrates the advantages of consistently applying values in good and bad economic conditions. This company, which was hived off from Hewlett-Packard, has managed to maintain its position as an employer of choice despite having to make pay cuts and redundancies, as shown by its rankings in the *Sunday Times* and *Fortune*'s 'best companies to work for' lists in 2002. Agilent argues that this has been achieved through an employer of choice policy that goes beyond the recruitment stage to incorporate terms and conditions and

a strong commitment to training and development.

◘ In Abbey National, the HR team is responsible for considering the relationship between branding and people management. The Abbey National Group has developed an employment proposition that is based on the principle that all employees are partners in the business. This proposition includes offering flexible and family-friendly working and external initiatives focused on the wider community. The HR team has taken an evidence-based approach to the employment proposition that has included commissioning academics to analyse the impact of the proposition on some key staff, and how the company is perceived in the internal and external labour market.

◘ Chapter 4 concludes that brand performance is strongly influenced by people management and development strategies, including the consistent pursuit of employer of choice policies and the extent to which an organisation can successfully communicate an employment proposition to its workforce. However, this relationship is adversely affected by any incongruity between brand identity and employees' perception of the reality of the brand, and the brand's reputation.

◘ The report stresses that appropriate people management and development policies and practices are positively linked to strong brands, particularly at a corporate level. However, the authors argue that the relevance of HR for managing brand will vary according to organisational context. They outline a number of different levels at which this involvement occurs.

◘ The authors argue that the literature concerned with the psychological contract and that on employer of choice and employment branding has similar messages. However, the marketing-oriented discourse of the latter two might be more useful than the concept of the psychological contract to HR practitioners trying to engage colleagues from other functions. The report points to some of the drawbacks of a strong culture in organisations, and the reservations of some commentators to 'brandwashing' of employees, but concludes that senior management can influence organisational culture either positively or negatively. This underlies the approach that the report takes to the branding and HR relationship.

◘ A new language of branding and people management and development does not offer radical solutions to organisational problems, but the report concludes that it can lead to a new way for HR professionals to engage in the development of business strategy in their organisations.

1 | Introduction

The Coca-Cola brand has recently been estimated as worth just under $70 billion. As with many organisations, its branding policy is now the cornerstone of its business strategy, and serves as the single most important filter for assessing change. Building, or just as often defending, a corporate brand or reputation has become a major concern of organisations in industries as diverse as financial services, information and communications technology, retailing, hospitality, motor vehicle manufacture and higher education, healthcare and local government. In these industries it is generally acknowledged that having employees support the brand is vital, yet this is an issue on which the human resources (HR) literature, particularly in the UK and Europe, is almost silent, with few direct references to the branding-HR relationship.

Three trends suggest that the importance of branding is unlikely to be short-lived:

◘ the high-profile nature of corporate and global branding

◘ the development of the services-based economy in all advanced economies

◘ the growing importance of intangible assets and intellectual capital as sources of strategic advantage.

The overall aim of this report is to make connections between two distinct bodies of knowledge:

◘ the externally-oriented marketing research on branding issues

◘ the internally-oriented, largely practitioner-based literature on the role of employees and human resource management in the branding process.

By doing so, the report aims to help people management and development professionals to better understand the brand management process, and to increase their influence with those responsible for creating and managing brands.

Outline of the report

Over the past decade, there has been an expanding volume of marketing literature that has sought to establish connections between brand advantage, customer service and how people are managed. This work is most convincing in setting out a more fine-grained picture of different notions and trends in branding (de Chernatony, 2001; Harris and de Chernatony, 2001) and corporate reputation management (Davies *et al*, 2003), but deals only superficially with the people management issues of culture, psychological contracts, communications, recruitment and selection, employee development and performance management and retention. Yet, with some minor exceptions (eg Ewing *et al*, 2002; Hatch and Schultz, 2001; McEwen and Buckingham, 2001), a search of accompanying HR databases has produced surprisingly little work that makes explicit reference to the branding–HR relationship.

This lack of apparent concern, especially among HR academics, is surprising, particularly because of the increasing service element in developed countries, with the focus of many companies on the employee–customer service–profit chain (Heskett *et al*, 1997). In addition, there is evidence that organisations in the UK, Europe and the USA are involving HR practitioners in the brand management process (eg Royal Bank of Scotland Group, Arriva, Hilton Hotels, Deutsche Bank), and

> **'…a search of…HR databases has produced surprisingly little work that makes explicit reference to the branding–HR relationship.'**

of the emergence of specialist consulting firms which offer services on employment branding, such as Versant.

One can only speculate on the possible reasons for this lack of a current, well-developed, evidence-based HR literature. Such reasons would undoubtedly include:

- the compartmentalisation of thinking in UK industry and the business schools, rooted in old-style functions and disciplines

- the lack of desire among many HR academics on this side of the Atlantic to engage with practice or to write in a style that engages practitioners, and

- the perhaps more justifiable belief of HR academics that there is little new in this relationship beyond the prescriptions of the 1980s culture-excellence literature and the more recent versions of the psychological contract literature, which focuses on the role of communications.

However, HR practitioners potentially have much to offer in the branding process. This is based on the evidence of four streams of academic and practitioner-based HR literature that collectively inform the branding–HR relationship, sometimes implicitly and sometimes explicitly reinforcing the message that 'it all happens from people' (Peters and Waterman, 1982). These four streams are:

- the culture-excellence literature, including the classic work by Schein (1985) on the external adaption–internal integration problem, the 'In search of excellence' literature of the early 1980s recently revisited by Colville, Waterman and Weick (2001), the more academic and

critical literature on culture management (Martin, 1992; Willmott, 1993, Ogbonna and Harris, 2002), and new derivatives, such as the work of Hatch and Schultz (2001)

- the 'new' strategic management or 'resource-based view' (RBV) that focuses on the relationship between strategic advantage and internal resources and intangible assets such as people and knowledge (Barney, 1991; Grant, 1991; Boxall, 1995; Boxall and Purcell, 2003)

- the employer of choice literature and consulting practice, which arises out of the work in the 1990s on the emergence of new psychological contracts (Rousseau, 1995; Guest, 1998). This work focuses on the belief by some employers that, faced with the changing circumstances of the 1990s, and their difficulties in maintaining old-style psychological contracts based on job security, there was a need for them to become employers of choice to retain the levels of trust, commitment and identity necessary for doing effective business (Cappelli, 1995). Such arguments have led employers to think more closely about the connections between satisfied employees, customer satisfaction, branding and financial performance

- the largely consulting-based employment branding literature and practice (Ewing *et al*, 2002), which deals most obviously with issues of branding and attempts to use branding and marketing concepts to align employees behind strong corporate and line brands.

The report thus examines the importance of branding and brand management for HR and assesses the future of branding and its implications for people management. Chapter 2 reviews the

> **'This work focuses on the belief by some employers that...there was a need for them to become employers of choice to retain the levels of trust, commitment and identity necessary...'**

literature on marketing and HR to determine what can be learned about the branding–HR relationship and the different functions performed by branding and brand management, and to assess the pressures for change towards corporate branding. It also reviews the four streams of organisational and HR literature and consulting practice as they apply to the branding–HR relationship.

Chapter 3 draws on two case study companies that demonstrate different aspects of the relationship between branding and HR. These case studies have been written on the basis of interviews with senior HR staff and company material. The companies are Agilent Technologies, which has recently split from Hewlett-Packard and is known for its strong employer brand and

employer of choice strategy, and Abbey National, one of the leading European financial services organisations.

Chapter 4 constructs some preliminary models of the relationships between branding and HR, with a view to developing propositions and raising questions that might guide future research. The models also serve as a practical guide to HR managers in working with marketing staff. Chapter 4 also examines some key themes raised by our review of the literature, including its usefulness beyond the level of a new language for HR, the problems of best practice prescriptions, and the assumptions made by this literature on the nature of organisational culture and change management.

2 | Linking the branding, HR and management literature

Defining brand

Product and service-level branding have played a significant part in the marketing strategy of firms for many years, but it is the increased importance of corporate and global brands that has caused organisations to think more closely about their external brand image and corporate reputation, and how their employees identify with and actively support the brand (Berthon, Hulbert and Pitt, 1999; Davis, 2001; Hatch and Schultz, 2001; Harris and de Chernatony, 2001; Davies *et al*, 2003).

This is not to say that such developments are new, since there are strong brands still evident from 50 years ago in the top 100 global brands, such as Coca-Cola, Hewlett-Packard, Gillette, Volkswagen and Kellogg's (Anon, 2002a). This longevity reflects the power and functions of brands in building long-term trust in companies, increasing customer loyalty and convincing consumers of the benefits of products and services. Branding helps reduce customers' search costs for perceived high-quality products and services and also conveys with it certain psychological rewards, as Berthon, Hulbert and Pitt (1999) point out. For suppliers, branding also helps to ensure repeat purchases, assists in the development of new product launches, facilitates market segmentation by communicating directly to the intended customers of the product or service, and facilitates premium pricing.

This report is concerned primarily with corporate branding, but this is not the only way of thinking about the idea of brand. For example, de Chernatony (2001a; 2001b) has explored some of the differing interpretations held by brand managers about branding, a number of which have immediate relevance for HR and people management. These interpretations include brands as:

- visual logos and signifiers, which foster differentiation among customers

- legally-enforceable statements of ownership – eg among the ancient or prestige universities

- branding companies, which reduces the need to promote individual lines of business or products, and is seen increasingly as a way of engaging new and existing employees in the corporate brand

- a form of shorthand for consumers which reduces the information-processing limitations of individuals and helps them to give attributes to products and services

- reducing the risk for customers in imperfect markets

- positioning by helping to associate brands with particular benefits for customers

- personality, in which brands are infused with emotional values beyond their functional benefits

- a relationship builder, which is an extension of the idea of brands as embodying a personality into the notion of customers having a relationship with the brand

- clusters of values which help organisations extend into new markets with related values

- added value beyond the basic product or service offered, for which customers are usually willing to pay a premium price

Figure 1 | Interpretations of branding and the links with HR

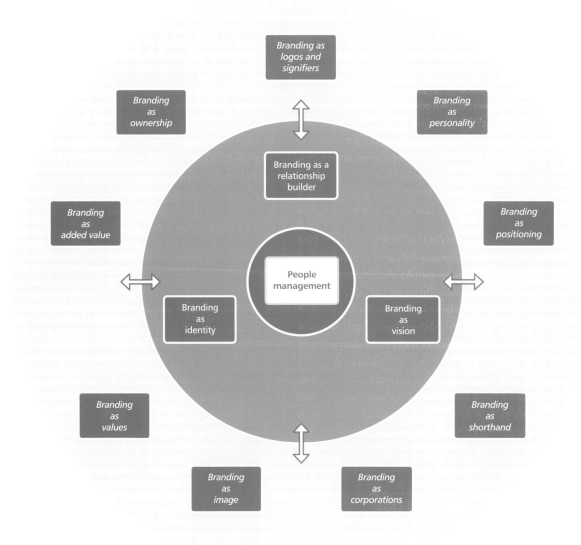

Source: based on de Chernatony (2001b).

> **'It is widely recognised that satisfaction with service brands is intimately related to the…behaviour of employees…'**

- ◻ visions that are used mainly to galvanise stakeholders into actions designed to attain some future desired state

- ◻ identity that sets out an ethos with which organisational stakeholders can readily associate

- ◻ image, which focuses on what customers perceive to be real.

It can be seen from these diverse interpretations that the brand managers in this study viewed branding as playing not only a key external role in adapting their organisations to market circumstances, but also an important internal role in aligning people behind the brand.

In Figure 1, we have adapted de Chernatony's (2001b) ideas to construct a representation of the internal and external views on branding.

Of the 13 roles of branding identified above, at least three are strongly internally focused and have major implications for people management and HR professionals. It should also be noted that there is a clear link between people management, the employee-focused definitions of branding and the externally-focused definitions.

This way of looking at branding through the language of marketing specialists provides a clear message for HR specialists who wish to make claims for their inclusion in key strategic decisions (Boxall and Purcell, 2003) and is one of the central arguments of this report. In this way, HR practitioners may find that engaging with the powerful discourse of branding may help them make the connections between HR and business performance.

Connecting the branding literature and HR

There has been a trend in the marketing literature towards incorporating people management issues in branding decisions and in brand management (Berthon, Hulbert and Pitt, 1999; de Chernatony and Dall'Olmo Riley, 1999; Ewing *et al*, 2002; Harris and de Chernatony, 2001). Such work has been a feature of the services marketing literature (Gronroos, 1994), especially in the area of service branding (de Chernatony and Dall'Olmo Riley, 1999).

Because one of the key aspects of services marketing and relationship marketing is the inseparability of production and consumption, common to all of this literature is the alignment of internal people-related policies, systems and practices with marketing services. It is widely recognised that satisfaction with service brands is intimately related to the expected and perceived behaviour of employees, which is often the most difficult factor to control in the marketing mix.

However, this literature is rooted in the belief that communications are the main source and solution for all organisational problems. It tends to restrict the role of HR to communicating brand values, rather than being the source of such values and the driver of key aspects of strategy.

Harris and de Chernatony's (2001) model illustrates these points. Their starting ground is the need for employees to become 'brand ambassadors' in their role as the key interface between the internal and external environment of the organisation and in having a potentially powerful influence on customers' perceptions of the brand offering and the corporation. These two authors attempt to bring together a number of the different interpretations of brands listed above to explain the concept of brand identity, which they define as

an organisation's ethos, aims and values that create a sense of individuality which differentiates a brand.
Harris and de Chernatony (2001, p.442)

Figure 2 shows that brand identity comprises the connections between an organisation's core vision and culture, positioning in the marketplace, the emotional or personality characteristics of potential customers, its presentation styles, and the consistency between employee relationships and customers.

However, the authors argue that a brand's identity is not always the same as its reputation, which they define as 'a collective reputation of a brand's past actions and results' (p.445) that describes its

ability to deliver value to key stakeholders. The authors regard brand reputation as more important in establishing and measuring brand performance, precisely because reputation takes into account the *past* as well as the *present* and it also encompasses all organisational stakeholders.

It is thus this key development in branding – away from an emphasis on products to a focus on corporate-level branding and corporate reputation management (Davies *et al*, 2003) – that has caused organisations to think more inclusively about how front-line customer service staff, designers and developers, knowledge workers and a range of other employees can influence brand reputation. Moreover, corporate branding requires consistency and uniformity in delivering the brand identity by all members of the brand management team and other stakeholders, including customers and employees.

So we are beginning to see clear causal connections made between key people management issues, employer of choice and employment branding, brand performance and the strategic goals of viability and sustained competitive advantage that nearly all commercially-oriented organisations pursue (Boxall and Purcell, 2003).

The culture-excellence literature

As we noted in Chapter 1, HR academics may have overlooked the branding–HR relationship because at one level at least it can be seen as little more than 'old wine in new bottles'. There is little doubt that the marketing literature, with some exceptions, seems to have caught up with the 'culture-excellence' literature, which has dominated much of management thinking and practice during the 1980s and 1990s.

Figure 2 | The relationships between brand identity and brand reputation

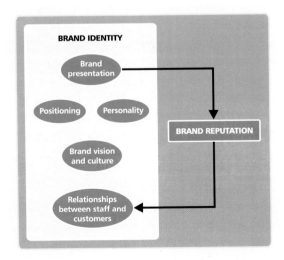

Source: based on Harris and de Chernatony (2001, p 443).

> '...the managerially-oriented "optimistic" literature on culture
> management...provides the rationale for the current focus on strategic HR...'

This body of work, which began with Peters and Waterman (1982), fuelled the idea that the search for business success began with a serious examination of the internal images of organisation. Their book *In Search of Excellence* promoted the message that

the environment of most organisations was largely and increasingly uncontrollable, that the 1970s focus on 'outside-in', rational management techniques was therefore misplaced and meaningless, and that feelings and people (ie culture) were what mattered most.

Colville, Waterman and Weick (1999).

Consequently, excellence was achieved through a strong emphasis on customer focus, which, they argued, 'all began from people'.

This focus on culture as a source and driver of success has resurfaced over the past two decades and has influenced many of the 'business guru' writers, such as Pascale (1991), Kotter and Heskett (1995), and Collins and Porras (1996), and has contributed to the emergence of 'new strategic management' as a body of thought which focuses on internal resources as the key driver of competitive success (see the Strategic management literature section, p.10).

In a more balanced presentation, Schein (1992) usefully outlines the problem of organisations as

one of simultaneously managing external adaptation to the changing environment of organisations with internal integration, which requires aligning and controlling human resources.

Such management of dualities, paradoxes and tensions has become a key feature of the change

literature, which, as Ruigrok *et al* (1999) have pointed out, lies at the heart of successful new ways of working in general.

The culture-excellence literature has, however, been roundly criticised for its over-emphasis on the internal workings of the organisation to the detriment of markets (Porter, 1996), the use of culture as a variable that is in the gift of managers to control (Martin, 1992) and, from an ethical standpoint, by critical management writers (Du Gay and Salaman, 1997; Legge, 1995; Willmott, 1993; Ogbonna and Harris, 1998).

We return to these criticisms in chapter four – but the managerially-oriented 'optimistic' literature on culture management has had an unquestionable influence on the practice of many organisations and provides the rationale for the current focus on strategic HR, with its emphasis on vision and values.

In the context of the branding–HR relationship, the most modern and direct derivative of this work on organisational culture is by Hatch and Schultz (2001), who have conducted research on 100 companies in the USA and Europe with a view to establishing a strong relationship between 'corporate image, corporate vision and organisational culture'. By 'image' they mean the outside world's or stakeholder impression of the company, including that of customers, shareholders, the media and the general public. 'Vision' refers to what senior managers aspire to for the company, while 'culture' refers to the organisation's key values, behaviours and attitudes (p.130).

They have argued that to build an effective corporate brand, organisations must ensure that these three elements of an organisation – which they call the 'three strategic stars' – must be aligned. According to these authors, misalignments occur when there are significant gaps between the 'stars':

◻ The *vision–culture gap* results when senior managers move the company in a direction that employees either do not understand or do not support. Sometimes this is a consequence of the pace of change, in which the vision is too stretching. At other times it results from visions that sit uneasily with ethical or traditional values, such as the attempted re-branding of the Post Office to Consignia. The gap is often referred to as the 'rhetoric–reality gap' (Legge, 1995).

◻ The *image–culture gap* usually results when organisations do not put into practice their brand values, and leads to confusion among customers about the company's outside image. This gap is generally most apparent when employees' views of the company are quite different from those held by customers.

◻ The *image–vision gap* occurs when there is a mismatch between the external image of the organisation and senior management's aspirations for it. The example that Hatch and Schultz (2001) use is the attempt by British Airways to globalise its image by removing the Union Jack from its tailfins. These actions led to a major public and press reaction, a cabin-crew strike and threats by key customers to switch to different carriers.

Hatch and Schultz (2001) have developed a framework (or 'toolkit') that comprises a series of diagnostic questions to assess the extent of misalignment between these three 'strategic stars' (see Figure 3). These questions do not break new ground in assessing culture, but point to the complex relationships between the external and internal aspects of managing effective corporate branding, placing equal weight on these dimensions.

The strategic management literature

A second important stream of literature is the 'new strategic management' or resource-based view of the firm (Barney, 1991; Grant, 1991; Barney, 2002). This approach has developed as a counter to the traditional 'outside-in' approaches, in which the starting point for thinking about strategic management and competitive advantage is the external environment. The work of Michael Porter is most associated with this outside-in perspective.

The resource-based view on strategy and, by extension, on HRM sees the fundamental – and indeed, only – sustainable route to competitive advantage as arising from how you put together unique and enviable combinations of internal resources – of which the most important is people and their relationship to other key systems in the organisation, such as knowledge and information (Boxall, 1996; Boxall and Purcell, 2003).

Such a perspective has led some writers to argue that how organisational cultures are managed and how employees are selected, developed, rewarded and organised is what differentiates firms, especially in knowledge-based industries or the growing service sectors in Europe and the USA (Pfeffer, 1998; Thurrow, 1999). The resource-based view thus has strong links with humanist ideas on learning organisations and organisational learning (Easterby-Smith, Crossan and Nicolini, 2000).

Like the earlier outside-in approaches, however, these 'inside-out' theories have in common a tendency to offer a one-best-way solution,

Figure 3 | The corporate branding toolkit

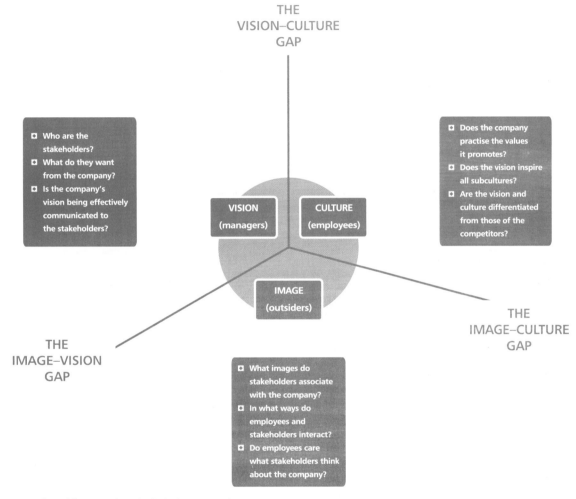

Source: adapted from Hatch and Schultz (2001, p131).

regardless of context, and to proselytise employees at the expense of other aspects of the business (Argyres and MacGahan, 2002; Porter, 1996). In effect, as Porter (1996) has suggested, resources themselves are of no competitive value, which is determined more by how and in what context such internal resources are used.

However – as both camps are beginning to recognise – the answer to this fundamental question on competitive strategy probably lies somewhere in the middle, such that both perspectives have something to offer (Boxall and Purcell, 2003). Nevertheless, the resource-based view has managed to 'rebalance the debate',

> '...another stream of influential strategic management literature...is based on the notion of core internal competences...and the complementary idea of the "balanced scorecard".'

grounded on the rationale that you don't move a seesaw by sitting in the middle.

This view has also provided a major intellectual and empirical justification for HR and its links to key strategic decisions on issues such as branding.

Consistent with the resource-based view of the firm, another stream of influential strategic management literature has begun to explain effective and sustainable strategic advantage. It is based on the notion of core internal competences (Hamel and Prahalad, 1994; Hamel, 1998) and the complementary idea of the 'balanced scorecard' (Kaplan and Norton, 1996; 2001).

The balanced scorecard is particularly relevant to the links between HR and branding, since it makes explicit and very practical links to balancing the needs and measurement of satisfying customers and financial objectives with the effective management and measurement of internal business processes, including people, and individual and organisational learning and growth.

In their most recent book, Kaplan and Norton (2001) have also developed a strategy map or 'theory of the business', which is, in summary, a cause-and-effect model to help managers understand the relationships between critical performance drivers and their associated outcomes.

Especially in the context of service industries, such as retailing and financial services, there have been a number of important contributions that link the marketing of services and customer satisfaction to internal market and human resource management (Loveman, 2001; Pugh *et al*, 2002). The best known of these is the employee–customer service–profit chain identified by the Sears corporation in

the USA (Heskett *et al*, 1997; Kirn *et al*, 1999) (see Figure 4).

Hemmington and Watson (2002) have made similar links in their research into the hotel industry. Drawing on the service–profit chain and related concepts from marketing, they have argued that the service encounter provides the best and probably only unique opportunity to differentiate service to individual customers, thereby creating higher levels of customer satisfaction and repeat business. The delivery of employee-centred actions were more important than the marketing literature of hotels, which in promising high levels of customer service, often through vague and clichéd statements, failed to differentiate between hotels and had the negative potential to over-promise that which could not be delivered.

Further evidence on the central nature of the service encounter has been reported by McEwen and Buckingham (2001). They discuss the results of a recent Gallup poll in the USA of six major sectors on the factors that influence brand performance, which found that for all sectors the single most important factor in building brand loyalty was employee behaviour. In the case of the airline industry, interaction with employees was three times more powerful than any other factor, including product performance.

On the negative side, poor employee performance was also important in customer dissatisfaction, particularly when there were no other features to differentiate among products or services.

Employer of choice

During the 1990s an important stream of literature emerged on the 'new psychological contracts' (Rousseau, 1995; Guest, 1998), based on the need

Figure 4 | The employee–customer–profit chain at Sears

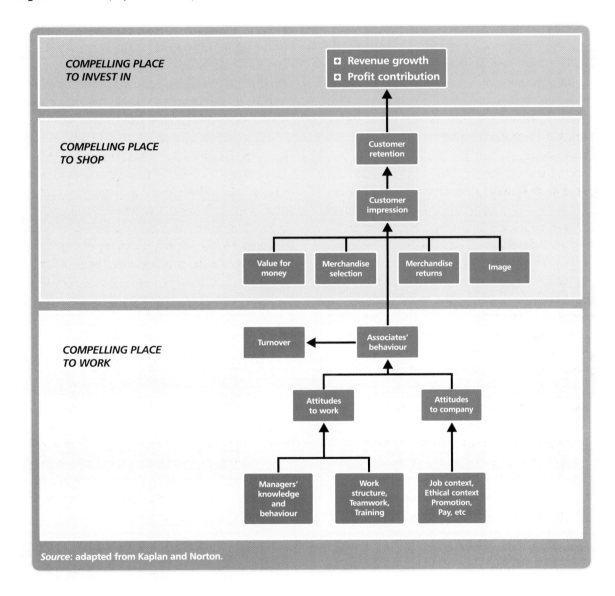

Source: adapted from Kaplan and Norton.

> 'For some organisations, following an employer of choice strategy means little more than more sophisticated and sensitive recruitment practices…'

to become an employer of choice (Cappelli, 1995; 1998). This argument served as an antidote to the business process re-engineering, de-layering and downsizing exercises undertaken by many organisations during the early part of the 1990s, and led employers to think more closely about the connections between employee satisfaction and retention, hiring, customer satisfaction, branding performance, financial performance and corporate performance.

According to consultants such as Ahlrichs (2000) and Ashby and Pell (2001), becoming an employer of choice is a deliberate business strategy which has driven some large US and UK employers to benchmark themselves against others in rankings of 'The Best Place to Work', published by *Fortune* magazine in the USA and *The Times* in the UK.

Although such ideas and strategies have their roots in a decade of unprecedented economic growth in the USA, when recruitment and retention were among the most important business issues for American employers (Stein, 2000), they appear not to have diminished in importance since the economic downturn following the winter of 2000/ 2001. To the extent that the UK has managed to escape the worst excesses of the slowdown in economic growth, it is all the more likely that UK organisations, faced with problems of recruitment, motivation and retention, will consider such approaches to be an essential part of their competitive strategies.

For some organisations, following an employer of choice strategy means little more than more sophisticated and sensitive recruitment practices, such as improving recruitment design, online recruitment, sensitive induction, retention analysis, cafeteria compensation and benefits, and 'growing your own' talent (Ahlrichs, 2000; Konrad and

Deckop, 2001; Tarzian, 2002). For others, it means a new, more contextually sensitive version of the old-style relational psychological contract (Cappelli, 1998) in which long-term commitment from employers – demonstrated through the organisation's goals, values and trust initiatives – is matched by high-commitment and low-turnover responses from employees.

Such a psychological contract is characterised by highly competitive remuneration and benefits, often including elements of contingent pay, interesting, challenging and varied projects, a commitment to training and development tailored to individual needs, flexible working arrangements, family-friendly policies and a motivating work environment.

This consulting recipe for an employer of choice strategy is highly reminiscent of the influential work by Pfeffer (1998), in which he identified seven practices of highly successful companies from his review of US and European literature. The list encompassed prescriptions on:

- employment security

- selective hiring

- self-managed teams and decentralisation

- high compensation contingent on organisational performance

- extensive training and development

- reduced status distinctions

- extensive information sharing on performance and financial issues.

'Employment branding has been defined as the "company's image as seen through the eyes of its associates and potential hires"...'

Contrary to some of the ideas that were fashionable during the 1990s, which advocated changes in the terms of the traditional psychological contracts to a new, transactional employment contract based on employability and no long-term commitment to individual careers inside of an organisation (eg Capelli, 1998), Pfeffer made it a central part of his argument that employment security provided the necessary 'table stakes' for the implementation of other high-performance work practices.

He reviewed a number of studies that showed the negative consequences of downsizing, including important connections between downsizing and the adverse impact on organisational performance, and including powerful negative correlations between employee turnover and positive assessments of customer service, which is a vital factor in establishing and maintaining strong brand identities.

If downsizing had to be undertaken, Pfeffer (1998) argued that it could be accomplished sensitively and sensibly, in a way that retained the morale of those surviving and minimised the impact on the company's image in concurrent and future hiring campaigns.

The employment branding literature

This final stream of literature deals most obviously with issues of branding and attempts to use branding and marketing concepts to align employees behind strong corporate and line brands (Murphy, 2000; Ewing *et al*, 2002; Shackell, 2002; Sichelman, 2000). However, as we shall argue, there are strong similarities between this work and the newer versions of the psychological contract literature.

Over the past few years, the concept of employment branding has entered into the lexicon of HR specialists and particularly consultants. US firms such as Versant offer an employer branding toolkit to engage employee loyalty and build organisational commitment. Perhaps the most complete study to date of employment branding is the US Conference Board's work (Dell and Ainspan, 2001), which surveyed and undertook follow-up interviews with executives in 137 major US companies.

This study found that employees were becoming a much more important target for corporate image-makers, although they did not necessarily use the term 'employment branding'. Forty per cent of respondents reported using the methods of corporate branding in their attempts to attract, retain and motivate employees.

Other less systematic evidence has reported a fast-growing interest among European companies such as Philips, Siemens, Fiat and Deustche Bank in the idea of employer branding (Anon, 2001). Such an interest is closely associated with the concept of brand risk, which results when investors perceive a threat to their brand brought about by poor brand management, concurrent with the increased perception that poor employee performance can be most damaging to a brand image and reputation (McEwen and Buckingham, 2001).

Employment branding has been defined as the 'company's image as seen through the eyes of its associates and potential hires', and is intimately linked to the 'employment experience' of 'what it is like to work at a company, including tangibles such as salary and intangibles such as company culture and values' (Ruch, 2002, p.3). Like the minimalist version of the employer of choice, much of the content of employment branding programmes emphasises the traditional HR activities of attraction, recruitment, motivation and retention, and there is little new in the way of advice to HR practitioners from this consultancy-dominated literature. For example, Table 1 below contains the lists of do's and don'ts from the consulting literature.

Reminiscent of the 'strategy-as-compelling-narrative' approach that has become popular in the strategic management literature (Barry and Elmes, 1997; Martin and Beaumont, 2001), the key questions appear to be:

◘ What is the compelling and novel story that we can tell people about working here?

◘ How do we tell the story to potential and existing employees in a way that convinces them of the reality of what we have to offer?

The difference seems to lie in the message and the methods of communicating the message.

Summary

So far we have seen that the marketing literature has begun to make explicit references to the management of people, in tandem with the developments in corporate and global branding as a key element of the overall strategy of many organisations. We have also noted how HR literature and practitioner thinking has begun to take the issue of branding seriously and, in some cases, to adopt the language of branding as a way of making connections with the strategic marketing function.

In the next chapter we discuss two case studies of organisations that illustrate different aspects of the relationship between branding and HR.

Table 1 | Lessons from employment branding consultants

McKenzie and Glynn (2001, pp22–26): Ten recommendations for communicating an employee brand	Govendik (2001, pp 4–9): Engaging employees to define the brand at Lante	Ruch (2002): Empoyer brand evolution – a guide to building loyalty in your organisation (Versant Consulting)
Get consistent – build a layer of a few key messages that can be reinforced by facts	Find the company from within, by surfacing the brand image through the eyes of employees	Assess your company culture using the cultural elements survey
Recognise what is not part of the message to be communicated	Create a brand vision and brand attributes or values that will ring true with brand ambassadors	Construct an appropriate employer brand identity that can be marketed externally and internally
Understand the key moment of truth in the recruitment process, especially the point at which people would accept an offer. Make this as early as possible	Roll out the brand by compelling employees to understand the brand, their responsibilities in making the brand live, and by getting them excited and engaged in the brand roll-out	Develop an employer brand promise which describes the value proposition to employees
Know what's compelling about the organisation, especially for high performers	Gain employee buy-in through consistent education and training	Develop an employer brand voice, a tool for ensuring consistent communications with associates
Understand the 'brand promise', particularly which elements are non-negotiable	Reinforce key brand attributes by giving employees first crack of the whip in giveaways, gifts, etc, associated with the roll-out of the brand	Implement the brand promise, using the brand voice and integrated communications tools
Work *with* employees to ensure that there is consistency in the story	Define the brand as part of the organisational culture by creating a constant stream of stories and events designed to support the key brand attributes	Measure the employer brand effectiveness, using a specially constructed index in key areas such as recruitment, retention and motivation
Design collateral information to make the truth compelling		
Ensure that intermediaries have the same story and work on your behalf		
Do not allow any intervention to pass without reinforcing the message of the employment brand		
Ensure that your internal change efforts are in line with your emerging employment brand		

3 | Case study evidence

In the following two case studies we have drawn on published material and interviews with senior HR staff to show how context and strategy influence the relationship between branding and people management. Our key messages from these cases are:

◘ There is no 'one-size-fits-all' policy on branding and HR, and different contexts and stages in the development of organisations require different branding–HR relationships.

◘ There are no quick fixes to becoming an employer of choice, but the benefits of achieving such a status can be incalculable during the inevitable bad times.

◘ It makes good business and HR sense to adopt an evidence-based approach in developing employment branding propositions and in measuring the effectiveness of these propositions.

Case study

Agilent Technologies: an employer of choice and an employment brand leader in difficult circumstances

Agilent Technologies is an excellent illustration of a company pursuing a consistent employer of choice strategy through good and bad times, and of a company that has sought to take the notion of employment branding seriously. This company features many of the previously noted practices of successful companies (Pfeffer, 1998), many of the key practices associated with employment branding and the employer of choice literature, and also demonstrates how one company has used HR to sustain success in difficult times (CIPD, 2003).

Agilent Technologies is a major international company, formed as a spin-off from Hewlett-Packard (HP) in 1999. It operates in 40 countries throughout the world – more than half of its revenue is generated from outside the USA. The company has emerged from the original, non-computing product divisions of HP and specialises in the design, development, production and marketing of communications and life sciences technology, which includes wireless communications, semi-conductor products, test, measurement and monitoring devices and chemical analysis equipment. Agilent considers itself a knowledge-based enterprise: high levels of skills are required in research and development, production, marketing and management. It retains much of its HP heritage, and its corporate culture, values and ethics are a strong feature of the new company.

Interviews were held with the UK HR team, based at the company's major UK site at South Queensferry, near Edinburgh, from which we received a strong impression of an organisation that lives its global brand values of respect for individuals, even under very difficult market conditions. Following years of prosperity as a separate division of HP and early success as a new company, according to the HR staff, the market for its products had 'virtually collapsed' after the downturn in the US economy in early 2001. This market downturn, the severity and length of which had never been experienced while the company was part of HP, was 'uncharted territory' for all employees and had placed its employer of choice policy under considerable strain.

In March 2001, the company began a severe exercise in cost-cutting that included a temporary 10 per cent salary cut. Then in August 2001, Ned Barnholt, the chief executive officer, announced the first redundancies in the history of the company, either as part of HP or as the newly-formed Agilent.

A second round of redundancies in November resulted in a total of 8,000 employees and 5,000 temporary staff worldwide being laid off. Yet despite these difficult times

> **'Following years of...early success as a new company...this market
> downturn...placed its employer of choice policy under considerable strain.'**

for the company, Agilent still ranked number 39 in the 2002 *Sunday Times* annual list of The Best Companies to Work For in the UK. This list ranks companies on employees' responses to a survey of their employers, conducted by a third party. Agilent was also ranked third for work–life balance, 82.8 per cent of those surveyed saying they were encouraged to balance work with personal life. Finally, and perhaps most significantly, Agilent in the USA – where most of the cuts were felt – was also ranked 31 in *Fortune* magazine's The Best Companies to Work For in 2002.

In the light of this downsizing, how has the company retained its high rankings? The UK HR staff believe that such rankings are a product of consistency in the application of the company's values, and that they are reaping the rewards of a trust dividend created throughout its previous 60 years of operation.

The first point made by the HR team was that compulsory redundancies was the last option to be considered – cost-cutting and voluntary pay reductions were used to head off and curb the immediate need for downsizing. It was only when it became obvious that these measures were not going to be sufficient that redundancies were considered, and as a recent *Fortune* magazine article explained (Roth, 2002), they were handled with the utmost sensitivity.

For example, 3,000 managers in the corporation were sent to outplacement consultants to help their staff cope with the problems of redundancy. As a further example of the company's sensitivity to its brand values, it has also remained true to its employer of choice policy. As one HR manager explained:

The company has stuck with its employer of choice policy. An example is graduate hiring. A year or so ago we were recruiting 100 graduates a year and competing for top talent, along with a number of major firms in Scotland. We were competing in a very competitive market for software engineers, electrical engineers, etc.

Now there is no graduate hiring at all. As a consequence we were extremely worried that our reputation as a company might have suffered a little, so we have still been active in graduate fairs and the like, explaining why we haven't been taking people on, because we see the need to demonstrate our commitment to the market and we expect things to change. You cannot turn off and on like a tap; you need to be visible.

The employer of choice policy extends well beyond the hiring stage, as its rankings in the *Fortune* and the *Sunday Times* lists imply, for its employment conditions are rated among the best in Scotland. These include:

◻ performance-contingent pay

◻ flexible working hours

◻ group-wide bonuses, pensions and life assurance

◻ employee assistance programmes to help with stressful personal and domestic issues

◻ well-above-average holidays

◻ subsidised high-quality cafeterias

◻ excellent sports facilities.

Agilent is also heavily committed to training and career development, with a well-funded employee education assistance programme which provides support for training and education that can be justified for business reasons.

The HR managers also explained how HR had been involved in the corporate branding exercise, citing the tagline to the company name 'Agilent Technologies: Innovating in the HP way', which implied a major consideration of HR issues in the development of the brand name. They perceived themselves as part of an integrated company, comprising a team of managers

> '**They perceived themselves as...a team of managers and employees living the...brand values that balanced business and employee needs.**'

and employees living the Agilent brand values that balanced business and employee needs.

This was exemplified by the HR director, who saw no distinction between the external and internal role of branding.

We are a values-driven company and cannot operate in any other way. The corporate values are extremely important to us, both inside and outside the company. For example, we have this Standards of Business Conduct policy, in which we do business in a very different way from many other companies... We are a 60-year-old company with a history, the HP heritage, with policies that have stood us in good stead over that period. So we have a very high expectation of how people will behave externally and internally.

When asked whether employees in the UK were still 'living the brand', HR managers explained how the most recent employee survey results had surprised them.

Given all that has happened – 10 per cent and then 5 per cent pay cuts, bonuses not paid, redundancies for the first time ever – the [survey] results hardly changed. We were still good against our internal and external benchmarks. There has been a fall off, but not nearly as much as we expected. What has happened recently has been a shock to the organisation and a radical shift for many people, but the value proposition has still been compelling to most of them.

They also pointed out how 98 per cent of people in the UK company had volunteered for the first round of pay cuts as a way of lessening the impact of redundancies. This figure, however, was slightly less for the second round of pay cuts, indicating that it was not seen as a sustainable solution by employees or the company.

Policy within the company is still to benchmark against the best companies to work for, wherever it operates. The HR managers reported that Agilent aims to be in the top 20 *Fortune* and *Sunday Times* best companies and to retain their excellent rankings in listings in countries such as India and Australia, where it ranks very highly. This commitment to HR benchmarking, despite the current conditions, helps explain what actions are required to be an employer of choice and also explains how HR can support and drive the brand reputation.

Case study

The Abbey National Group: developing an evidence-based approach

The Abbey National Group (ANG) is one of the UK's best-known financial service companies and high street brands, and dates back to its formation following the merger of two building societies in 1989, although its origins go back to 1850.

The ANG became a plc in 1989 following the passing of the Financial Services Act in 1986, which placed limits on the ability of building societies to raise funds and offer services, and the 'Big Bang', which led to the breaking down of traditional barriers between banks as centralised lenders and other organisations who were offering a range of financial products and services.

At around the same time, the ANG embarked on a diversification policy away from its traditional mortgage business because of changes in the market environment, including the incursion of traditional banks into the mortgage market following the Big Bang and the maturing of the home ownership market in the UK, in which home ownership reached 67 per cent. In effect, more players were competing in a market that had little opportunity for natural growth.

Currently, the Group provides a comprehensive range of personal financial services including savings and investments, mortgages, banking, pensions, unit trusts, life and general insurance products and secured and

> '...the HR team is attempting to develop a consistent and measurable employee proposition across the Group...'

unsecured lending. Abbey National also has retail operations in France and Italy and offshore operations in Jersey, the Isle of Man, Gibraltar, Portugal, Hong Kong and Dubai. At the time of the research, these activities were organised in three major divisions, each with some well-known brand names:

◘ retail banking, including Abbey National, Abbey National Life, Abbey National PEP Managers Ltd, Abbey National Unit Trust Managers Ltd and Inscape Retail

◘ wholesale banking, including Abbey National Financial Products, Abbey National Treasury Services plc (a leading participant in the international financial markets), Cater Allen International Ltd, IEM Airfinance BV, and Porterbrook

◘ wealth management and long-term savings, which includes the Abbey National Banks in Italy and France, Abbey National Financial Investment Services, Abbey National Financial Investment Services Ireland, Abbey National Offshore, Cahoot (the recently formed Internet bank), Cater Allen Private Bank, City Deal, First National, Inscape, Inscape Offshore, James Hay Insurance Company Ltd, James Hay Investment Services Ltd, James Hay Pension Trustees Ltd, Scottish Mutual, and Scottish Provident.

The Group's strategic HR team is responsible for considering the branding–HR relationship and is beginning to do some interesting work in this area by pursuing an evidence-based strategy.

The ANG has a well-developed 'employment proposition', which is based on a set of values and practices that 'regard all our employees as partners in the business', and which

recognises, respects and values individual differences acknowledging the distinctive contribution that each person makes to business success.

(company website)

It also has a stated aim to be 'the financial services employer of choice in the UK', based on a policy of inclusion and diversity and

founded on the fundamental belief that all employees should be treated with equal openness, honesty and respect.

(company website)

Currently, the specific practices associated with the employment proposition are:

◘ flexible working – including part-time working, job share, career breaks – that allows employees to take time away from work for up to five years – a voluntary reduced working time scheme, under which employees can voluntarily reduce their working hours for a period of between six months and five years, term-time working, and a piloted teleworking scheme

◘ family-friendly practices, 26 weeks' maternity leave, returner's bonus payable to employees when they return to work after the birth of their baby, life-flex leave including parental leave and paternity leave, summer play-schemes, etc

◘ external initiatives, through national campaigns for minority and disabled groups, and local initiatives including partnerships with other employers to provide opportunities for school-leavers, undergraduates, minorities, and people with disabilities.

However, the HR team is attempting to develop a consistent and measurable employee proposition across the Group, which they see as varying along a continuum ranging from emotionally-based statements of what it is like to work at ANG to details of the employment offer package. As in a number of major organisations, they have used the concept of the psychological contract to develop a language for the employment proposition and as a means of measuring progress (Guest and Conway, 2002). Indeed, they have commissioned researchers at Birkbeck College to undertake a large-scale analysis of the employment proposition and its impact on financial advisers.

From other research carried out, they found that employees placed a very high value on their immediate work environment, which they have attempted to address as part of their revised employment proposition. This includes answering such questions as how the importance of the immediate work environment is expressed in the current employment proposition, how it is operationalised and measured, whether all groups in ANG express similar views concerning the work

environment, and which HR levers can be used to match employee expectations.

ANG is taking this evidence-based approach to developing its employment proposition and its employer of choice policy further by piloting research to identify how the employment proposition is currently perceived in the internal and external labour market for financial advisers. It is also proposing to undertake a study that attempts to elicit the differing views of senior HR staff and the marketing team responsible for developing the brands, with a view to bringing about a common view of what constitutes the brand and how it might best be communicated.

4 | Discussion and conclusions

In this chapter, we attempt to bring together the various ideas from the literature and some of the case study evidence to shed light on the branding–HR relationship.

◘ First, we have constructed a causal model of the relationship between key features of HR and branding and drawn out some propositions for practitioners and researchers.

◘ Second, we have taken this model a little further and constructed a stage model of the branding–HR relationship, which might help HR practitioners think more closely about their ability to influence the branding process.

◘ Third, we have raised some issues that must be addressed by members of the HR community and future research.

Modelling the relationship between HR and branding performance

Drawing on our literature review and the cases, we can begin to model the relationship between HR and branding performance, as set out in Figure 5 on page 26. The core message of the model is that brand performance – as measured by consumer and employee evaluations as well as the more traditional business indicators – is causally linked to HR strategies in an organisation. These strategies include the extent to which the organisation sees its workforce as a driver of business success, pursues contingently appropriate and consistent employer of choice strategies, and develops and successfully communicates an employer brand identity or proposition to its employees.

This direct relationship, however, is mediated by two important factors:

◘ the perceived degree of congruence between the brand identity/proposition message of the brand team and employees' perceptions of the match between company rhetoric and reality (Harris and de Chernatony, 2001)

◘ the brand reputation – the collective representation of past and current actions that influence a brand's ability to deliver valued outcomes to multiple stakeholders (Harris and de Chernatony, 2001).

To make the model more comprehensive and realistic, we must include two other sets of factors that influence how the brand team and employees perceive the brand proposition. They are:

◘ The brand vision – does it tell a novel and compelling message? Is the brand vision aligned with the organisational culture, and does it present a credible message in the light of past action by the organisation?

◘ The brand team characteristics – to what extent does the brand team encompass different viewpoints from a range of stakeholders, including HR? To what extent do the brand team members agree on the brand proposition?

From this model we can begin to tease out some practical propositions and suggestions for further research that might lead to a more refined understanding of the HR and branding relationship, as shown below.

Figure 5 | The relationship between HR and brand performance

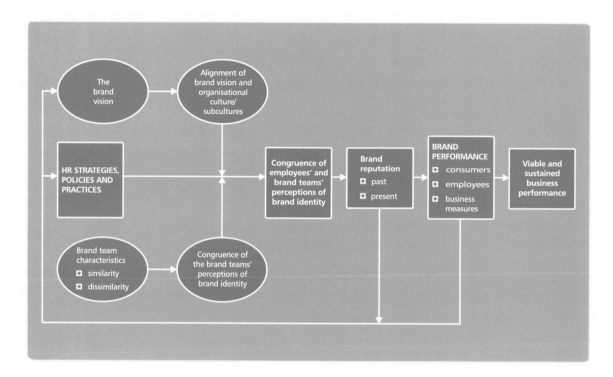

Propositions on the HR–branding relationship

Proposition 1

Employers who adopt a resource-based view of strategy, supported by the consistent application of an employer of choice strategy, will achieve a close alignment between employees and the brand team on the brand identity and value propositions.

Proposition 2

Employers who develop an appropriate employer brand identity and explicit set of value propositions, and communicate these effectively to employees, will achieve a close alignment between employees and the brand team on the brand identity and value propositions.

Proposition 3

Close alignment between employees and the brand team on the brand identity and value propositions will lead to a positive brand reputation, particularly when past actions support current organisational rhetoric on the brand message.

Proposition 4

The more brand reputation is subjected to comprehensive performance measurement,

> '...the sophisticated management of people is intimately connected to the development of strong, particularly corporate-level, brands...'

involving consumer, employee, operational and financial indicators, the greater will be the increase in brand value.

Proposition 5

Brand teams that have an appropriate balance of similar and dissimilar characteristics and experiences of marketing and HR will produce a greater degree of agreement on the brand identity and value propositions.

Proposition 6

The greater the level of agreement of the brand team on the brand identity and value propositions, the greater is the likelihood that employees will align with the brand message.

Proposition 7

The more the brand vision, which is senior managers' aspirations for the brand, is consistent with past managerial practices and actions, the greater the alignment between the vision and the organisational culture and subcultures will be.

Proposition 8

The more a brand vision contains a novel and compelling message for employees, which relates to employee values and aspirations, the greater the alignment between the vision and the organisational culture and subcultures will be.

Proposition 9

The greater the alignment between the brand vision and the organisational culture and subcultures, the closer the alignment between

employees and the brand team on the brand identity and its value propositions will be.

The future of the branding–HR relationship

The core message of our model in Figure 5 is that the sophisticated management of people is intimately connected to the development of strong, particularly corporate-level, brands. It has set out some relationships between important factors, the presence or absence of which will help or hinder effective branding performance.

However, the model also implies that some organisations will perceive a greater relevance than others for the role of HR in the branding process. In that sense it also implies a theory of stages in the relationship between branding and HR, which serves as a pointer to the future for organisations and specialists involved in the branding process.

If our model in Figure 5 serves as one key dimension of this stage theory, another dimension has been spelled out in a general explanation of branding in the financial services industry (Interbrand, 2002). This is the extent to which organisations differ in attaching importance to corporate branding in their general business strategy. By combining these two dimensions, we can describe at least four stages of development (see Figure 6 on page 29).

The first stage corresponds to the version of branding as a well-defined and protected signifier or logo for particular products, services or individual businesses, but in which HR plays little or no role in supporting the brand and where there is no attempt to connect individual brands to employees' motivations, values or behaviour. Such a stage is likely to describe the position of many smaller or newer companies, especially in the non-service sectors, which do not see brands as embodying values that can relate to customers or employees.

The second stage applies to organisations that may have a master brand as a logo but place more emphasis on building a vision and value proposition for existing or new product or service brands. This may be because of the strength of existing brand reputation or because they wish to launch a new line of business that is distinct from the values of the master brand – as in the case of Cahoot, the Internet arm of the Abbey National Group.

The role of HR in this context is to provide support for the individual brands, and the connection with employees' values is to identify with these individual brands. However, the potentially negative effects of such strategies, which are strong on product or service differentiation but weak on integration with the corporate values and cost-sharing in areas such as HR and IT, have led some companies to move to the third stage of development.

The third stage of development attempts to capitalise on the vision and values of a strong corporate brand for significant organisational change – for example, in bringing together previously disparate business operations, such as ABB in the late 1980s and early 1990s (Bjorkman, Belanger and Berggen, 1998), or in improving service offerings, such as Sears. The role of HR in providing support for this process of corporate branding lies in designing programmes for change, and the role of the corporate brand is to provide a compelling employment brand proposition for staff as well as to provide an identity for

customers. Although the payoff for such a strategy can be significant in having employees 'live the brand' and in building strong relationships with customers, such changes are difficult to implement universally and usually require many years to become fully embedded.

For example, in a number of cases we have studied over the past decade (Martin, Beaumont and Staines, 1998; Martin and Beaumont, 1999; Martin, Beaumont and Pate, 2003), top-down programmes of corporate vision and values change failed because the nature of the programmes and the style of brand leadership and means of communication were insensitive to context. Senior managers also attempted to impose tight deadlines for the changes, and, in one case, the deadline set was less than a year to inculcate a new set of corporate brand values.

Where companies succeed at this third level, they may move to the fourth stage of development, in which the corporate brand becomes the centrepiece of the overall strategy, HR plays a pivotal role in driving the corporate branding process, and employees identify closely with the corporate brand values and act as brand ambassadors. The role of individual product or service brands and employee identification with them is secondary, the recruitment and deployment of employees frequently being used to underpin the corporate branding strategy.

It is at this stage that employer of choice policies are most likely to be found – that employees are recruited, developed and rewarded for identification with the corporate brand as much as, or more than, for a specific job. The payoff to the organisation, in addition to having employees identify with existing business, is believed to be that employees will be more flexible and innovative

Figure 6 | A staged model of the relationship between branding and HR

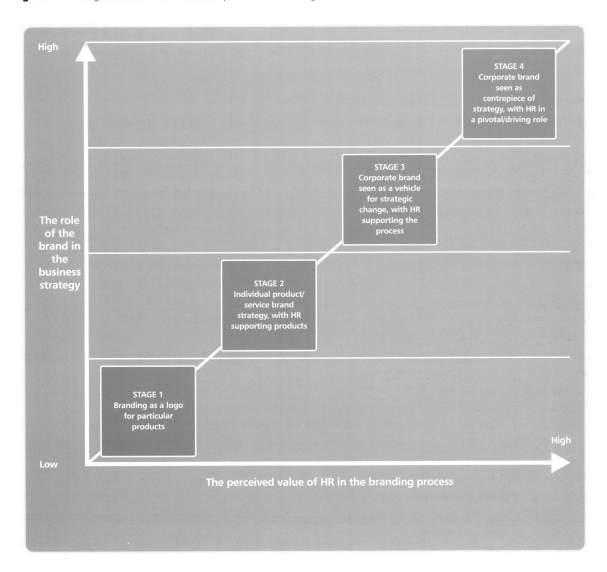

> '...the literature on employer of choice and on employment branding and...on the psychological contract...all three strands of work have their roots in the optimistic culture management school...'

in delivering future business or service improvements, or, as in the case of Agilent, be prepared to tough it out when the going gets rough.

However, a cautionary note must be added. Some development or stage theories usually involve a sense of progress and inevitability, and in that sense, come from the one-best-way or best practice school. We do not wish to imply any such linear thinking or assumptions, since our belief is that context and time-frames play an important part in shaping the strategic positions of organisations. At most, stage theories can set out some 'promising practices', rather than best practice, regardless of circumstance, and ours is no different.

Unfinished business

HR academics and practitioners might be struck by the close parallels between the literature on employer of choice and on employment branding and the more recent work on the psychological contract, which places a heavy emphasis on the explicit message and the nature of communications. This should come as no surprise, since all three strands of work have their roots in the optimistic culture management school, which we deal with below.

For example, Guest and Conway (2002) have recently surveyed 3,000 CIPD members to ascertain the extent to which the concept of the psychological contract was used by them to manage employment relations and the content of the psychological contract, which, in its explicit version, closely mirrors the notion of an employer brand value proposition or promise, and the high commitment work practices associated with the employer of choice literature (Pfeffer, 1998). They also looked at the range of HR practices used to

manage the contract, and the effectiveness of the various types of communication used to deliver the contract.

Guest and Conway (2002) found that:

◻ More than a third of respondents make explicit use of the new language of the psychological contract in managing employment.

◻ Communications play a significant role in managing psychological contracts. The evidence supported the notion that more explicit versions of a contract, setting out expectations and obligations, result in increased fairness and trust, and a reduction in perceived breaches of the contract.

◻ The different forms of communications have different effects, recruitment-related communication and job-related communication (eg through targets, appraisal, briefing, informal and formal training, etc) proving to be more effective in contract delivery and acceptance than top-down communications through mission statements and annual senior management presentations.

◻ Senior managers – the focus of the study – admitted to often, either partly or completely, failing to keep their promises and commitments to employees – ie their part of the psychological contract.

Although the language of this work is more refined, its messages are essentially similar to those of the employer of choice and employment branding literature. It might thus be argued that we have two competing discourses essentially dealing with similar concepts and propositions: the employment branding/employer of choice

> **'The most compelling feature of this optimistic version...is the promise of a rare and inimitable way of competing.'**

literature, which has its origins in the marketing, communications and HR consulting industry, and the more analytical, psychological contract literature, which has become popular with academics, and increasingly also with UK practitioners.

However, the marketing-based discussions on employment branding may have more value to HR professionals because it speaks across key functions, and it is more focused on an increasingly critical issue in developing business – the subject of branding. In addition, it reaches outwards to the customer and inwards into the emotional intelligence, needs and perceptions of workforce. It should come as no surprise that HR consultants with an eye to the main chance should have hijacked such a powerful marketing discourse to deal with the implementation of vision statements. They may find it more appealing than the theoretically sound but arguably complicated and less focused language of the psychological contract on specific outcomes such as brand reputation.

Culture management

We need to deal with the assumptions underlying culture management, the principal tool for employment branding.

In one of the most recent reviews of the organisational culture literature, Ogbonna and Harris (2002) promoted the idea of three perspectives – the 'optimistic', 'pessimistic' and 'realistic' versions. The optimistic version, which underpins nearly all of the branding–HR literature and much of the other literature we have discussed, is premised on the notion that strong leadership, promoting a vision and values

framework, can create a unitary corporate culture, which aligns the majority of organisational members behind the vision and motivates them in a way no other management technique can hope to achieve (see, for example, Kotter and Heskett, 1995). The most compelling feature of this optimistic version, in line with the arguments of the resource-based view on strategy, is the promise of a rare and inimitable way of competing.

Such a version of corporate culture management has been challenged by the – mainly academic – pessimists, who spell out four major objections.

The first is the assumption that organisational culture can be controlled, which, as a number of theorists have argued, is difficult if not impossible. Instead, they see culture as something that mainly exists and operates at the deepest levels of human consciousness, which managers cannot fully understand and are thus incapable of manipulating, except at the most insignificant surface levels.

The second objection concerns the way in which the optimists assume that cultures emerge and change. For example, Martin (1992), Willmott (1993) and others are highly critical of the assumption that senior managers should have a monopoly over the value system of an organisation and that the reality of most organisations is of conflicting and contradictory subcultures or highly fragmented organisations that cannot be said to have a culture at all in the strict sense of the term. The optimistic search for shared values and meanings is thus unlikely ever to be fully realised, except among mangers at the apex of the organisation.

The third objection is an ethical one: so, for example, some writers (Willmott, 1993; Legge,

> '...it is clear to us...that in certain circumstances an organisation's culture can be shaped...by managerial actions, and that leadership can have a...role in this process.'

1995) take issue with the social engineering and manipulative aims of 'culture managers'. Such an objection is made explicit in the critical use of the term 'brandwashing' to describe the negative aspects of employment branding in cases like Starbucks (Reese, 1996). For instance, it has been pointed out by Schein, one of the founders of the culture management school, that his early work was undertaken on the brainwashing of US prisoners during the Korean War.

The fourth objection is elaborated by Morgan (1997) and others (eg Kets de Vries, 1989 and Miller, 1992) as the 'dark side of culture'. These writers point to the 'psychic prison' effects of strong cultures and powerful but dysfunctional leadership that can limit the vision of managers and inhibit much-needed change by creating dysfunctional boundaries and rigidities, 'groupthink' and 'cognitive traps'. Pascale (1991) followed this line of reasoning in explaining how organisations in the 1980s came to grief because 'nothing failed like success', which was brought about by years of strong but inflexible cultures that trapped managers into outmoded ways of seeing and acting.

This health warning from the critics of culture management serves as an important antidote to the rather naïve and overly rational view of the optimists, and, by extension, to those writers and practitioners who see employees as capable of being branded or brandwashed into accepting ideas that are not in their interests. Yet it is clear to us from previous research that in certain circumstances an organisation's culture can be shaped, but not necessarily controlled, by managerial actions, and that leadership can have a positive but also negative role in this process (Martin and Beaumont, 2001; Martin, Beaumont and Pate, 2003).

Ogbonna and Harris (2002) have described those authors that take a position on organisational culture, which 'is neither in support nor against the management of organisational culture' (p.26), as 'realists'. Such realism is based on the position that neither the optimists nor the pessimists can provide complete explanations of how cultures can and do change, and that, in certain circumstances, such change can be both necessary and beneficial to a majority of employees.

It is from such a perspective that we view this notion of employer branding and the branding–HR relationship. Undertaken sensitively and treating employees as genuine stakeholders in the process, the often competing aims of all organisational members may be reconciled and advanced.

Best practice or best fit? The weakness of rational management approaches

Nearly all of the literature we have reviewed is predicated on the assumption of unitary goals – such as brand performance or maximising shareholder value – as the overarching aim of organisations. Secondly, there is a strong undercurrent of the values of the rational planning and design school of strategic human resource management (Whittington, 2000). As a consequence, much of the literature and practice is heavily prescriptive and does not deal adequately with the relationship between strategy, branding and HR in practice.

In the strategic HR literature there are two schools of thought that exemplify this tradition – the best practice and strategic fit schools (Boxall and Purcell, 2003).

Best practice HR, as Boxall and Purcell (2003) have argued, has been most enthusiastically received by

> **'The best fit approaches have tended to dominate the academic, rather than practitioner, literature on HRM.'**

American practitioners and academics. This model comes in three different guises (Wood, 1999): high-commitment management, high-involvement management, and high-performance management.

As we have noted, the work by Pfeffer (1998) on the seven practices of successful organisations is one of the standard examples and most widely cited texts in the USA. In the UK, David Guest's work on strategic HR and the psychological contract is also based on the belief of the superiority of high-involvement HR and the importance of integrating HR systems into the broader business strategy of the organisation.

Although this literature has empirical support, four rather obvious criticisms are usually levelled at the best practice school.

- The first is the issue we have already dealt with above concerning the neglected role of power, and begs the question: 'Best practice – in whose interests?'

- The second concerns the role of national or business system contexts (Boxall and Purcell, 2003), for – as many researchers have pointed out – HR practices tend to be embedded in particular contexts and are not easily transferable between different business systems and cultures.

- The third concerns the issue of whose list you use, because – as some writers have pointed out – they have a tendency to differ according to sector and organisational context (Woods, 1999).

- The fourth is a more practical one and raises the question: 'If the medicine is so potent and so obvious, why isn't everyone taking it? Where is the competitive advantage in doing what everyone else can do?' The best fit school offers some answers.

The best fit approaches have tended to dominate the academic, rather than practitioner, literature on HRM. Perhaps the best-known of these best fit approaches was the attempt by Schuler and Jackson (1987) to locate appropriate HR strategies and their behavioural implications in the competitive strategy framework developed by Porter (1985). We have already developed the resource-based-view critique of Porter's rather static view of strategy.

However, best fit is not solely concerned with the relationship between HR systems and strategy (external fit), but also with two other kinds of internal fit. One has to do with the fit or degree of integration of HR policies and practices, to avoid what has been labelled 'deadly combinations'. The second involves the relationship between an organisation's HR policies and practices (its HR system) and other key organisational policies and practices on, for example, culture management or branding. One of the central issues for best fit proponents is thus to create synergies between HR policies and practices and between HR systems and other organisational systems (internal integration), and between HR systems and the competitive alignment of the firm, including its brand reputation (external adaptation).

Yet, as Wood (1999) points out in his extensive literature review on the links between HRM and performance, whether treated as a form of universal best practice or more contingently as in the best fit model, the literature remains focused on the direct impact of high-involvement or high-performance HR on organisational performance. In

> '...our model...incorporates a number of...mediating variables...adding a necessary complexity to the relationship between HR practices and brand performance.'

making this direct link, such work has lost its earlier focus and sophistication on the intervening role of social psychological factors as intervening variables, although the work of Guest (1998) and Purcell and others (CIPD, 2003) has attempted to remedy this deficit by incorporating the psychological contract as a mediating variable between HR practices and organisational performance.

We hope that our model in Figure 5, which incorporates a number of similar mediating variables, performs the same function in adding a necessary complexity to the relationship between HR practices and brand performance.

A second assumption of both best practice and best fit schools of thought is that high-involvement or employer of choice models of HR are a radical break with old-fashioned, Taylorist or human relations approaches to work organisation. Clearly, as we hope we have demonstrated, this is not the case. Contingent pay has strong links with Taylorism, as does sophisticated recruitment and selection. Moreover, culture management, teamworking and family-friendly policies have strong roots in the old human relations models and welfare tradition of personnel management (Rose, 1975; Niven, 1967).

To the extent that neither school of thought – scientific management nor human relations – was a break with its past or a complete solution to industry's ills at the time, we cannot expect a new language of branding and HR to offer radical solutions to organisations or the HR profession. However, our message is that it offers the opportunity for HR managers to engage with a powerful marketing and strategic discourse.

References

AHLRICHS N. S. (2000)

Competing for Talent: Key recruitment and retention strategies for becoming an employer of choice. Palo Alto, CA, Davies-Black Publishing.

ANON (2001)

'Building employer brands', *Business Europe, 41* (10), 1–3.

ANON (2002a)

'The 100 top brands', *Business Week*, 5 August, 77–80.

ANON (2002b)

'Is this Europe's best bank?', *Business Week*, 29 July, 32–33.

ARGYRES N. *and* MACGAHAN A. M. (2002)

'An interview with Michael Porter', *Academy of Management Executive*, 16 (2), 43–45.

ASHBY F. *and* PELL A. R. (2001)

Embracing Excellence: Become an employer of choice to attract the best talent. New Jersey, Prentice Hall.

BARNEY J. (1991)

'Firm resources and sustained competitive advantage', *Journal of Management*, 17 (1), 99–120.

BARNEY J. (2002)

'Strategic management: from informed conversation to academic discipline', *Academy of Management Executive*, 16 (2), 53–58.

BARRY D. *and* ELMES M. (1997)

'Strategy retold: toward a narrative view of strategic discourse', *Academy of Management Review*, 22 (2), 429–52.

BARTLETT C. *and* GHOSHAL S. (1998)

Managing Across Boundaries: The transnational corporation. New York: Random House Business Books.

BATES S. (2001)

'Use branding to drive home your message to employees', *HR Magazine*, 46 (December) 12, 14–20.

BERTHON P., HULBERT J. M. *and* PITT L. F. (1999)

'Brand management prognostications', *Sloan Management Review, 40*, Winter, 53–65.

BJORKMAN T., BELANGER J. *and* BERGGEN C. (EDS) (1998)

Producing Beyond Frontiers: ABB and the meaning of being local worldwide. New York, Cornell University Press.

BOXALL P. (1996)

'The strategic HRM debate and the resource-based view of the firm', *Human Resource Management Journal, 5* (5), 5–17.

BOXALL P. *and* PURCELL J. (2003)

Strategy and Human Resource Management. Basingstoke, Hants, Palgrave Macmillan.

CAPPELLI P. (1995)

'Rethinking employment', in R. S. Schuler and S. E. Jackson (eds) *Strategic Human Resource Management*, Oxford, Blackwell.

CAPPELLI P. (1998)

The New Deal at Work: Managing the market-driven workforce. Boston, MA, Harvard Business School Press.

CAULDRON S. (1999)

'Brand HR', *Workforce, 78* (11), 30–34.

CIPD (2003)

Sustaining Success in Difficult Times: Research summary. London, CIPD.

COLLINS J. *and* PORRAS J. (1996)

Built to Last: Successful habits of visionary companies. London: Century.

COLVILLE I. D., WATERMAN R. D. *and* WEICK K. E. (1999)

'Organizing and in search of excellence: making sense of the time in theory and practice', *Organisation*, 6 (1), 129–148.

DAVIES G., CHUN R., DA SILVA R. V. *and* ROPER S. (2003)

Corporate Reputation and Competitiveness. London, Routledge.

DAVIS S. (2001)

'Corporate branding: making the brand the strategic "driver" for an entire organisation', *Business Week*, August.

DE CHERNATONY L. (2001a)

From Brand Vision to Brand Evaluation. Oxford, Butterworth Heinemann.

DE CHERNATONY L. (2001b)

'The diverse interpretations of brands', *The Marketing Review*, 1, 283–301.

DE CHERNATONY L. *and* DALL'OLMO RILEY F. (1999)

'Experts' views about defining service brands and the principles of service branding', *Journal of Business Research*, 46, 181–192.

DELL D. *and* AINSPAN N. (2001)

Engaging Employees Through Your Brand. Conference Board Report, Number R-1288-01-RR, April. Washington D.C., Conference Board.

DU GAY P. *and* SALAMAN G. (1997)

'The culture of the customer', *Journal of Management Studies*, 29 (5) 615–633.

EASTERBY-SMITH M., CROSSAN M. *and* NICOLINI D. (2000)

'Organisational learning: debates past, present and future', *Journal of Management Studies*, 37 (6), 783–796

EVANS M. (2001)

'The best brand customers are your employees', *Marketing (UK)*, 19 April, 1–3.

EWING M. T., PITT L. F., DE BUSSY N. M. and BERTHON P. (2002)

'Employment branding in the knowledge economy', *International Journal of Advertising*, 21 (1), 3–23.

GOVENDIK B. (2001)

'Engaging employees to define the brand at Lante', *Strategic Communications Management*, 5 (2, Feb/Mar), 14–19.

GRANT R. (1991)

'The resource-based view of competitive advantage: implications for strategy formulation', *California Management Review*, 33 (2), 114–135.

GRONROOS C. (1994)

'From scientific management to service management: a management perspective for the age of service competition', *International Journal of Service Industry Management*, 5 (1), 5–20.

GUEST D. E. (1998)

'Is the psychological contract worth taking seriously?', *Journal of Organisational Behaviour*, 19, 649–664.

GUEST D. E. and CONWAY N. (2002)

'Communicating the psychological contract: an employer perspective', *Human Resource Management Journal*, 12 (2), 22–38.

GUNASEKRA C. (2002)

Employer branding – The perils of transdisciplinary extension. Paper presented at the British Academy of Management Annual Conference, 9–11 September, Kingston University.

HAMEL G. (1998)

Leading the Revolution. Boston, MA, Harvard University School Press.

HAMEL G. and PRAHALAD C. K. (1994)

Competing for the Future. Boston, MA, Harvard Business School Press.

HARRIS F. and DE CHERNATONY L. (2001)

'Corporate branding and corporate brand performance', *European Marketing Journal*, 35 (3/4), 441–456.

HATCH M. J. and SCHULTZ, M. (2001)

'Are the strategic starts aligned for your corporate brand?', *Harvard Business Review*, February, pp.129–134.

HEMMINGTON and WATSON S. (2002)

'Managing customer expectations – the marketing communications vs service delivery conundrum', *International Journal of Hospitality Management*.

HERRIOT P. and PEMBERTON C. (1996)

'Contracting careers', *Human Relations*, 49 (6), 757–790.

HESKETT J. L., EARL W. and SCHLESINGER L. (1997)

The Service Profit Chain. New York, New York Free Press.

HIRSCHORN K. (2001)

'Brands must be as attractive as your best friend', *Marketing (UK)*, 10 November, pp.1–3.

INTERBRAND (2001)

'Aligning your organisation and your brand for performance', *Interbrand Insights,* No. 3, March.

INTERBRAND (2002)

'Bank on the brand', *Business Papers*, No. 1.

KAPLAN R. and NORTON D. (1996)

The balanced scorecard: Translating strategy into action. Boston, MA, Harvard Business School Press.

KAPLAN R. and NORTON D. (2001)

The strategy-focused organization. Boston, MA, Harvard Business School Press.

KETS DE VRIES M. (1989)

'Leaders who self-destruct: the causes and cures', *Organisational Dynamics*, 17 (4), 4–18.

KIRN S. P., RUCCI A. J., HUSELID M. and BECKER B. (1999)

'Strategic human resource management at Sears', *Human Resource Management,* 38 (4), 329–335.

KONRAD A. M. and DECKOP J. (2001)

'Human resource management trends in the USA: challenges in the midst of prosperity', *International Journal of Manpower,* 22 (3), 269–278.

KOTTER J. P. and HESKETT J. L. (1995)

Corporate Culture and Performance. New York, Free Press.

LEGGE K. (1995)

Human Resource Management: Rhetorics and realities. Basingstoke, Macmillan.

LOVEMAN G. W. (1999)

'Employee satisfaction, customer loyalty and financial performance: an empirical examination', *Journal of Service Research*, 1 (1), 18–21.

MCEWEN B. and BUCKINGHAM G. (2001)

'Make a marque', *People Management,* 17 May, pp.40–44.

MCKENZIE A. and GLYNN S. (2001)

'Effective employment branding', *Strategic Communications Management*, 5 (4), 22–26.

MCLUHAN R. (1999)

'Motivating forces for a brand boost', *Marketing (UK)*, 30 September, pp.47–48.

MARTIN G. *and* BEAUMONT P. B. (1999)

'Thinking globally and acting locally: implementing culture change in ABB (Dundee)', in Bjorkman T., Belanger J. and Berggen C. (eds), *Producing Beyond Frontiers: ABB and the meaning of being local worldwide*, New York, Cornell University Press.

MARTIN G. *and* BEAUMONT P. B. (2001)

'Transforming multinational enterprises: towards a process model of strategic HRM change in MNEs', *The International Journal of Human Resource Management*, 10 (6), 34–55.

MARTIN G., BEAUMONT P. B. *and* PATE J. (FORTHCOMING)

'A process model of strategic change and some case study evidence', in Cooke W. (ed.), *Multinational Companies and Transnational Workplace Issues*. Westport, Conn, Quorum Press, pp.95–118.

MARTIN G., BEAUMONT P. B. *and* STAINES H. J. (1998)

'Managing a culture', in Mabey C., Clark T. and Skinner D. (eds), *Experiencing HRM*, Sage.

MARTIN J. (1992)

Cultures in organizations: Three perspectives. New York: Oxford University Press.

MILLER D. (1992)

'The Icarus paradox: how exceptional companies bring about their own downfall', *Business Horizons*, 35 (1) 24–36.

MINTZBERG H. (1999)

'Educating for the unknowable: the infamous real world', in Waddock S. (chair), *Transforming Management Education for the 21st Century: Changing and developing for global (and local) citizenship in a pluralistic world*. Symposium conducted at the Annual Conference of the Academy of Management, Chicago.

MITCHELL P., KING, J. *and* REAST J. (2001)

'Brand values related to industrial products', *Industrial Marketing Management*, 30, 415–425.

MORGAN G. (1997)

Images of Organisation. London, Sage.

MUDAMBI S. MCD., DOYLE P. *and* WONG V. (1997)

'An exploration of branding in industrial markets', *Industrial Marketing Management*, 26, 433–446.

MURPHY C. (2000)

'Instilling workers with brand values', *Marketing (UK)*, 27 January, pp.31–32.

NIVEN M. (1967)

Personnel Management 1913–1963. London, Institute of Personnel Management.

OGBONNA E. *and* HARRIS L. C. (1998)

'Managing organisational culture: compliance or genuine change?', *British Journal of Management*, 9 (2), 273–288.

OGBONNA E. *and* HARRIS L. C. (2002)

'Managing organisational culture: insights from the hospitality industry', *Human Resource Management Journal*, 12 (1), 33–53.

O'REILLY N. (2002)

'Battle of store brands starts the shopfloor', *Personnel Today*, 3 December, p.2.

PASCALE R. (1991)

Managing on the Edge. London, Penguin.

PERSONNEL TODAY (2002)

'Deutsche Bank seeks "flexible" employer brand', *Personnel Today*, 26 February, p.4.

PETERS T. *and* WATERMAN R. (1982)

In Search of Excellence. New York, Harper & Row.

PFEFFER J. (1998)

The Human Equation. Boston, MA, Harvard Business School Press.

PORTER M. E. (1985)

Competitive Advantage: Creating and sustaining superior performance. New York, Free Press.

PORTER M. P. (1996)

'What is strategy?', *Harvard Business Review*, November-December, 61–71.

PUGH S. D., DIETZ J., WILEY J. W. *and* BROOKS S. M. (2002)

'Driving service effectiveness through employee-customer linkages', *Academy of Management Executive*, 16 (4), 73–84.

REED S. (2002)

'Is this Europe's best bank?', *Business Week*, 29 July, pp.32–33.

REESE J. (1996)

'Starbucks: inside the coffee cult', *Fortune Magazine*, 134 (11), 190–197.

ROSE M. (1975)

Industrial behaviour: Theoretical developments since Taylor. London, Penguin.

ROTH D. (2000)

'How to cut pay, lay off 8,000 people, and still have workers who love you: It's easy just follow the Agilent way', *Fortune Magazine*, 22 January.

ROUSSEAU D. E. (1995)

Psychological Contracts in Organisations. Thousand Oaks, CA, Sage.

RUCH W. (2000)

'How to keep Generation X employees from becoming X-employees', *Training and Development Journal*, 40, April.

RUCH W. (2002)

'Employer brand evolution: a guide to building loyalty in your organisation', available at http://www.versantsolutions.com

RUIGROK W., PETTIGREW A. W., PECK S. and WHITTINGTON R. (1999)

'Corporate restructuring and new forms of organizing: evidence from Europe', *Management International Review*, 2 (Special issue), 41–64.

SCHEIN E. (1985)

Organizational Culture and Leadership. San Francisco, Jossey-Bass.

SCHULER R. and JACKSON S. E. (1987)

'Linking competitive strategies and human resource management practices', *Academy of Management Executive*, 1 (3), 207–219.

SHACKELL S. (2002)

'Brand champions will be rewarded', *Personnel Today*, 3 December, pp.22–24.

SICHELMAN L. (2000)

'Branding effort must touch employees', *National Mortgage News*, 25 (7), 30 October, 36-40.

SMIRCICH L. (1983)

'Concepts of culture and organisational analysis', *Administrative Science Quarterly*, 28, September, 339–358.

STEIN N. (2000)

'Winning the war to keep top talent', *Fortune*, 141 (11), 132–133.

STRAUSS G. (2001)

'HRM in the USA: correcting some British impressions', *The International Journal of Human Resource Management*, 12 (6), 873–897

TARZIAN W. (2002)

'Linking the hiring process to brand management', *Strategic HR Review*, 1 (3, March-April), 22–25.

THURROW L. (1999)

Creating Wealth: New rules for individuals, companies and countries in a knowledge-based economy. London, Nicholas Brealey.

WHITTINGTON R. (2000)

What Is Strategy, and Does It Matter? (second edition) London, Routledge.

WILLMOTT H. C. (1993)

'Strength is ignorance; slavery is freedom: managing culture in modern organisations', *Journal of Management Studies*, 30 (4), 515–552.

WOODS S. (1999)

'Human resource management and performance', *International Journal of Management Reviews*, 1 (4), 367–413.